NICOTEXT

Stand-Up

DO NOT DRINK AND DRIVE & DO NOT DRINK ALCOHOL
IF YOU ARE UNDER DRINKING AGE!

AND KIDS, REMEMBER, ALWAYS WEAR A CONDOM!

The publisher and authors disclaim any liability that may result from the use of the information
contained in this book. All the information in this book comes directly from experts but we do
not guarantee that the information contained herein is complete or accurate. The Content of
this book is the author's opinion and not necessarily that of Nicotext. This book is a collection
of quotes from various free websites and is not a reflection of a specific artists work, but
intended solely as a compilation of the concept of stand-up and stand-up artists throughout
time.

No part of this book may be used or reproduced in any manner whatsoever without the
written permission, except in the case of reprints of the context of reviews.
For information, email info@nicotext.com

Copyright ©NICOTEXT 2008 All rights reserved.
NICOTEXT part of Cladd media ltd.
ISBN: 978-91-85869-22-0
Printed in Poland

When in doubt,
go for the dick joke.

- Robin Williams

Chris Rock

Born:
February 7, 1965, in Andrews, South Carolina, USA.

Career:
Rock began doing stand-up comedy in 1985. In 1990, he became a cast member of Saturday Night Live and in 1991, he released his first comedy album. At this point, he was also acting in a few TV-shows and films, such as Miami Vice, Beverly Hills Cop and New Jack City.

Rock left Saturday Night Live in 1993, and did his first HBO comedy special the following year. Rock has also been in Comedy Central's Politically Incorrect.

He was voted by Comedy Central as the fifth greatest stand-up comedian of all time.

Do you know what the good side of crack is? If you're up at the right hour, you can get a VCR for $1.50. You can furnish your whole house for $10.95.

I live in a neighborhood so bad that you can get shot while getting shot.

Who's judging American Idol?
Paula Abdul?
Paula Abdul judging a singing contest is like Christopher Reeve judging a dance contest!

The only acting you ever see at the Oscars is when people act like they're not mad they lost. Nicole Kidman was smiling so wide, she should have won an Emmy at the Oscars for her great performance.

I was like, 'If you'd done that in the movie, you'd have won an Oscar, girl!'

You know the world is going crazy when the best rapper is a white guy, the best golfer is a black guy, the tallest guy in the NBA is Chinese, the Swiss hold the America's Cup, France is accusing the U.S. of arrogance, Germany doesn't want to go to war, and the three most powerful men in America are named 'Bush', 'Dick', and 'Colon.'
Need I say more?

Never go to clubs with metal detectors. Sure it feels safe inside. But what about all those niggas waiting outside with guns? They know you ain't got one.

Actually, I think all addiction starts with soda. Every junkie did soda first. But no one counts that. Maybe they should. The soda connection is clear. Why isn't a presidential commission looking into this? Or at least some guys from the National Carbonation Council.

George Bush hates midgets.

John Cleese

Born:
October 27, 1939, in Weston-Super-Mare, UK.

Career:
Cleese went to Cambridge to study law, but spent a lot of time in a performing group at the university. After finishing his studies, he started touring with the group and the show Cambridge Circus. After returning, he began a radio series on BBC and this is where the soon to be Monty Python and the Flying Circus was born.

Cleese wrote for and acted in the four Monty Python films: Monty Python and the Holy Grail (1975), Life of Brian (1979), Monty Python Live at the Hollywood Bowl (1982), and The Meaning of Life (1983).

Between the Monty Python films, Cleese also did the legendary TV-series Fawlty Towers.

Cleese has been in numerous films since, such as Harry Potter, James Bond and A Fish Called Wanda.

Oh, I could spend my life having this conversation
- look - please try to understand before one of us dies.

I find it rather easy to portray a businessman. Being bland,
rather cruel and incompetent comes naturally to me.

The trouble with the British is that they are not interested in
ideas. If Jesus came back today and offered to speak for
an hour on British television, they would say, 'What! Another
talking head?'

If God did not intend for us to eat animals, then why did he
make them out of meat?

Johnny Carson

Born:
October 23, 1925, in Corning, Iowa, USA.

Died:
January 23, 2005, in Los Angeles, Califorina, USA.

Career:
Carson started his career as a radio announcer and a television comedy writer. He then continued hosting several television quiz shows before he started doing The Tonight Show in 1962.

Carson stayed on that show for a whopping 30 years and became the icon for late night television. Carson is considered one of the most influential television performers, he has received no less than five Emmy awards and an American Comedy Lifetime Achievement Award.

If life was fair, Elvis would be alive and all the impersonators would be dead.

Democracy means that anyone can grow up to be president, and anyone who doesn't grow up can be vice president.

I was so naive as a kid I used to sneak behind the barn and do nothing.

For three days after death hair and fingernails continue to grow but phone calls taper off.

If variety is the spice of life, marriage is the big can of leftover Spam.

When turkeys mate they think of swans.

Groucho Marx

Born:
October 2, 1890, in New York, New York, USA.

Died:
August 19, 1977.

Career:
Marx started his career performing as a boy singer with his brothers in the group Four Nightingales. The brothers later developed a successful comedy act that went on Broadway and later became a movie.

In the 1930's and 1940's, Marx worked as a radio comedian and radio show host on a radio quiz program entitled You Bet Your Life. During the 1950's and 1960's he switched to TV instead, performing in TV-series such as Tell It To Groucho and Groucho. Marx did a one-man show during the 1970's, and released a double album; An Evening with Groucho.

Marx won an honorary Oscar in 1974.

I find television very educational. Every time someone turns on the set, I go into the other room and read a book.

Before I speak, I have something important to say.

Behind every successful man is a woman. Behind her is his wife.

I intend to live forever, or die trying.

I must confess, I was born at a very early age.

I worked my way up from nothing to a state of extreme poverty.

Marriage is a wonderful institution, but who wants to live in an institution?

Military intelligence is a contradiction in terms.

Outside of a dog, a book is a man's best friend. Inside of a dog it's too dark to read.

Those are my principles, and if you don't like them... well, I have others.

Tim Allen

Born:
June 13, 1953, in Denver, Colorado, USA.

Career:
Allen started his career when a friend dared him to try his luck onstage on a comedy night in a comedy club in Detroit. The performance went so well that it lead him to taking up stand-up comedy. Allen moved to Los Angeles and became a member of The Comedy Store. Allen performed at several late night talk shows and also did a Showtime television special: Men Are Pigs.

In 1991, he started doing the family sitcom Home Improvement, which was a big success for Allen and made him one of the 1990's most prominent comedians.

Women now have choices. They can be married, not married, have a job, not have a job, be married with children, unmarried with children. Men have the same choice we've always had: work or prison.

Men are liars. We'll lie about lying if we have to. I'm an algebra liar. I figure two good lies make a positive.

My mom said the only reason men are alive is for lawn care and vehicle maintenance.

Men are pigs. Too bad we own everything.

Playing golf is like going to a strip joint. After 18 holes you're tired and most of your balls are missing.

To get a man's attention, just stand in front of the TV and don't move.

Eddie Murphy

Born:
April 3, 1961, in Brooklyn, New York, USA.

Career:
Murphy started his career as a stand-up comedian as a 15-year old, by performing at local bars and clubs in New York. Murphy made his debut in Saturday Night Live in 1980. In 1982, Murphy received a Grammy nomination for an album of stand-up material.

Murphy left Saturday Night Live in 1984 and started working with films. He has been in films such as Beverly Hills Cop (1984), Coming to America (1988) Doctor Doolittle (1998) and Bowfinger (1999).

He was awarded a Golden Globe in 2007 and has received a numerous other prices.

I have nothing against homosexuals. I think an orgasm is your thing, and you should fuck whoever the fuck you feel like fucking. Whoever makes you come the hardest. Anybody who says you shouldn't, fuck them.

...then I watched the show, because I didnt really know him [Mr. T], I watched the show to see what kinda guy he was and the character on the show ain't too bright so I figured if he came upto me I could use the jedi mind trick on him:
Mr. T walks up to me and go 'I heard you did some jokes about me.'
'No you didn't.'
'Maybe I didn't...I'm gonna beat up the fool that gone tell me them lies.'

'Is this your bag sir?' Yeah, its my motherfucking bag! Why Motherfucker? A black man can't have a suitcase?!

Hey Eddie Murphy, Fuck You! I know you Eddie Murphy, its the 'Fuck you man'!

I was so mad I called Richard Pryor's house up and said 'Yo Richard, Bill Cosby just called me up and told me I'm too dirty', and Richard said,'The next time the motherfucker calls tell him I said Suck My Dick, cause I don't give a fuck. Whatever the fuck make the people laugh, say that shit.' He said, 'Do the people laugh when you say what you say?' I said 'Yes.' He said. 'Do you get paid?' I said 'Yes'. He said, 'Well tell Bill I said have a Coke and a Smile and shut the fuck up. Jello pudding eating motherfucker.'

Woody Allen

Born:
December 1, 1935, in the Bronx, New York, USA.

Career:
Allen dropped out of college and started working on NBC, where he wrote material for humor shows such as Sullivan Show and The Tonight Show. At the same time, he started doing stand-up on clubs in New York. Allen's comic art revolved around urban Jewish mentality.

In 1965, he left his stand-up career and did his first feature film: What's New, Pussycat? And Allen has kept producing films since, and is doing so to this day.
You recognize the theme in his films from his early career as a stand-up comedian.

I don't want to achieve immortality through my work...
I want to achieve it through not dying.

I can't listen to that much Wagner. I start getting the urge to conquer Poland.

I tended to place my wife under a pedestal.

I was thrown out of college for cheating on the metaphysics exam; I looked into the soul of the boy sitting next to me.

If only God would give me some clear sign! Like making a large deposit in my name in a Swiss bank.

Money is better than poverty, if only for financial reasons.

My one regret in life is that I am not someone else.

A fast word about oral contraception. I asked a girl to go to bed with me, she said 'no'.

Basically my wife was immature. I'd be at home in the bath and she'd come in and sink my boats.

I'd never join a club that would allow a person like me to become a member.

I will not eat oysters. I want my food dead. Not sick.
Not wounded. Dead.

I'd call him a sadistic, hippophilic necrophile, but that would be beating a dead horse.

Remember, if you smoke after sex you're doing it too fast.

Rowan Atkinson

Born:
January 6, 1955, in Consett, County Durham, UK.

Career:
Atkinson started his career with touring with Angus Deayton. After that, he did the TV-show Not Nine O'Clock News, which was a big hit. In 1983, Atkinson did the medieval sitcom The Black Adder, which became one of the most successful BBC situation comedies of all time.

Mr. Bean was born in 1990, and since then there has been numerous TV-series and movies about him. Atkinson has been listed in The Observer as one of the 50 funniest acts in British comedy.

As I was leaving this morning, I said to myself 'The last thing you must do is forget your speech.' And sure enough, as I left the house this morning, the last thing I did was to forget my speech.

You're about as useful as a one-legged man at an arse kicking contest.

A man may fight for many things. His country, his friends, his principles, the glistening ear on the cheek of a golden child. But personally, I'd mud-wrestle my own mother for a ton of cash, an amusing clock and a sack of French porn.

Jim Carrey

Born:
January 17, 1962, Newmarket, Ontario, Canada.

Career:
Carrey is said to have performed constantly as a child and in junior high, he allegedly kept small stand-up routines for his classmates every day.

After his stand-up debut in 1979, he moved to Los Angeles to pursue his career in comedy. Carrey auditioned to be a cast member for the 1980–1981 season of NBC's Saturday Night Live but was not selected.

Instead he started his TV and film career, and is today viewed as one of our times greatest comedy actors. He has received three Golden Globes.

Behind every great man is a woman rolling her eyes.

If I'm not back in five minutes... just wait longer!

My report card always said, 'Jim finishes first and then disrupts the other students'.

Maybe there is no actual place called hell. Maybe hell is just having to listen to our grandparents breathe through their noses when they're eating sandwiches.

There is nothing like making love to somebody you give a shit about.

Until Ace Ventura, no actor had considered talking through his ass.

Valentine's Day is a holiday invented by greeting card companies to make people feel like crap.

You know what the trouble about real life is?
There's no danger music.

Sacha Baron Cohen

Born:
October 13, 1971, in Hammersmith, London, UK.

Career:
Cohen attended Cambridge and after leaving the university, he started working as an actor in theatre. He later switched the theatre stage for TV and his career was launched in 1998 when his comic character and controversial alter ego Ali G was born. Ali G became an immediate hit with UK viewers and Cohen won Best Newcomer in the British Comedy Awards. In 2000, The Ali G Show started and the feature film Ali G In da house came out in 2002.

In 2006, the cinemas put on Cohen's second big character; Borat, in the mockumentary Borat: Cultural Learnings of America for Make Benefit Glorious Nation of Kazakhstan.

Cohen has won several awards, among others a Golden Globe in 2007 and has been nominated for Emmys a number of times.

Kazakhstan is more civilised now. Women can now travel on inside of bus, and homosexuals no longer have to wear blue hat.

In U.S. and A. they treat horses like we in Kazakhstan treat our women. They feed them two times a day. They have them sleep on straw in a small box. And for entertainment, they make them jump over fences while being whipped.

Sex can lead to nasty things like herpes, gonorrhea, and something called relationships.

Let's talk about some conspiracy things. Let's go back to the grassy knoll. Who actually shot J.R.?

Ali G: But what harm has violence ever done?
Media analyst: Oh... death!
Ali G: Yeah, but apart from that?

What's up? Being gay is the new coolest thing, which is why I came to gayest part of America, Alabama!

It is very strange that a woman can vote,
but a horse can not.

Tommy Cooper

Born:
March 19, 1921, in Caerphilly, Wales, UK.

Died:
April 15, 1984.

Career:
During the Second World War, Cooper was called up to serve as a trooper in Egypt. Cooper there became part of the entertainment party, and developed an act around magic tricks and comedy. This was the launch of Cooper's career and after leaving the army, he kept performing his comic art.

Cooper made his debut on BBC in 1948 and that's how he became known to the larger audience. Cooper did a large number of performances and worked as a comedian until the day he passed away. On April 15, 1984, Tommy Cooper collapsed from a massive heart attack in front of millions of television viewers. Cooper has been named England's funniest comedian at several occasions.

A blind bloke walks into a shop with a guide dog. He picks the Dog up and starts swinging it around his head. Alarmed, a shop assistant calls out: 'Can I help, sir?' 'No thanks,' says the blind bloke. 'Just looking.'

I used to be indecisive but now I am not quite sure.

It's strange, isn't it. You stand in the middle of a library and go 'Aaaaagghhhh' and everyone just stares at you. But you do the same thing on an aeroplane, and everyone joins in.

Last night I dreamt I ate a ten pound marshmallow.
When I woke up the pillow was gone.

Man goes to the doc, with a strawberry growing out of his head. Doc says 'I'll give you some cream to put on it.'

Apparently, 1 in 5 people in the world are Chinese. And there are 5 people in my family, so it must be one of them. It's either my mum or my dad. Or my older brother Colin. Or my younger brother Ho-Cha-Chu. But I think it's Colin.

Two cannibals eating a clown. One says to the other 'Does this taste funny to you?'

I went to buy some camouflage trousers the other day but I couldn't find any.

Dennis Miller

Born:
November 3, 1953 in Pittsburgh, Pennsylvania, USA.

Career:
Dennis Miller is one of the most famous stand-up comedians in the US. Miller started his career performing in clubs during the 1980's. His big break came in 1985 when he was the anchorman in Saturday Night Live in the Weekend Update and became famous for the phrase: 'That's the news, and I am outta here!'.

Miller got his own talk show in 1992; The Dennis Miller Show. The show was one of the first alternative shows and was cancelled because there were too few viewers. Two years later, he started Dennis Miller Live, a half an hour talk show on HBO. Miller and his staff won five Emmy Awards while hosting the show.

Besides being a stand-up comedian, Miller has also been an actor and a sportscaster.

In a nutshell, just be good and kind to your children, because not only are they the future of the world, but they are the ones who can eventually sign you into the home.

A recent police study found that you're much more likely to get shot by a fat cop if you run.

Guilt is simply God's way of letting you know that you're having too good a time.

The only way the French are going in is if we tell them we found truffles in Iraq.

I had a cab driver in Paris. The man smelled like a guy eating cheese while getting a permanent inside the septic tank of a slaughterhouse.

Jon Stewart

Born:
November 28, 1962, in Lawrenceville, New Jersey, USA.

Career:
Jon Stewart came out as a stand-up comedian in 1987. Two years later, he started working on TV. His TV-career started off at Caroline's Comedy hour, where he was a screenwriter and in 1992 he went on to MTV where he hosted You Wrote It, You watch It. The TV-series was short-lived, but in 1994 he developed his own TV-series for MTV and it became an instant hit: The Jon Stewart Show.

Stewart was in the running to take over David Letterman's old spot on NBC's Late Night in 1993, but lost out to the more experienced comic and writer, Conan O'Brien. In 1999, Stewart started hosting the satirical news show the Daily Show. Stewart has won ten Emmys for the Daily Show and is today seen as one of our times greatest comedians.

Thou shall not kill. Thou shall not commit adultery.
Don't eat pork. I'm sorry, what was that last one? Don't eat pork? Is that the word of God, or is that pigs trying to out-smart everybody?

I celebrated Thanksgiving in an old-fashioned way. I invited everyone in my neighborhood to my house, we had an enor-mous feast, and then I killed them and took their land.

I don't know what all the controversy is about, quite frankly. I've met Eminem, I met him backstage, and he's really gay.

I've been to Canada, and I've always gotten the impression that I could take the country over in about two days.

The Supreme Court ruled that disabled golfer Casey Martin has a legal right to ride in a golf cart between shots at PGA Tour events. Man, the next thing you know, they're going to have some guy carry his clubs around for him.

Ahh, Earth Day, the only day of the year where being able to hacky-sack will get you laid.

I know more about Bill Clinton's penis now than I do my own, which says something about the media or just something really sad about me.

This guy comes up and says, 'Are you Jon Stewart?' And I'm thinking, 'Oh, he's seen me on TV and wants my autograph.' But he asks me, 'So, do you have a beach badge? You need one if you're going on the beach.'
I think he just wanted to see if I had the $7 it took to buy a badge so he could have a story to tell years from now at the badge-checkers' bar.

I remember having a grade-school teacher I thought was a hard-ass. When you're that age, you think the guy is Himmler. Then you visit him eight years later and he's wearing polyester pants, he's four foot eight, you think he's gay, and you're like, 'Are you the guy I was afraid of?'

Eddie Izzard

Born:
February 7, 1962 in Aden, Yemen.

Career:
Izzard was born in Yemen, but grew up in England and on Ireland. He started his career as stand-up comedian as a street performer in Europe and the US during the 1980's. His first performance was at The Comedy Store in London, but the larger audience didn't discover him until the 1990's.

He toured with Live at the Ambassadors (1993), Unrepeatable (1994), Definite Article (1996), Glorious (1997) and Dress to Kill (1998) and in the end of the 1990's he also became well known to the American audience.

Eddie Izzard has won a great deal of awards, among them two Emmys and two Top Stand-up and Best Stand-up at the British Comedy Awards.

If you've never seen an elephant ski, you've never been on acid.

But with dogs, we do have 'bad dog.' Bad dog exists. 'Bad dog! Bad dog! Stole a biscuit, bad dog!' The dog is saying, 'Who are you to judge me? You human beings who've had genocide, war against people of different creeds, colors, religions, and I stole a biscuit?! Is that a crime? People of the world!'
'Well, if you put it that way, I think you've got a point. Have another biscuit, sorry.'

I grew up in Europe, where the history comes from.

I wanna live 'til I die, no more, no less.

I like my coffee like I like my women. In a plastic cup.

And the National Rifle Association says that, 'Guns don't kill people, people do,' but I think the gun helps, you know? I think it helps. I just think just standing there going, 'Bang!' That's not going to kill too many people, is it? You'd have to be really dodgy on the heart to have that...

I've done a bit of Latin in my time...but I can control it.

What shall we call our son so he does not get the shit kicked out of him at school? We shall call him Englebert Humperdink! Yes, that'll work.

Squirrels always eat nuts with two hands, always two hands, 'Raar-ra-ra-yum-yum-yum'. And occasionally they stop and they go (gasps, starts, then pauses and looks around, wide-eyed) As if they're going, 'Did I leave the gas on? (sudden happy realization) No! No, I'm a fucking squirrel!' (munching nuts).

Yes, no smoking in bars now, and soon there'll be, no drinking and no talking! Be careful, California, you're supposed to be the crazy state – out there, the wild ones. Soon everybody will be saying, 'Come down to the library, we'll have a wild time!'

We stole countries with the cunning use of flags. Just sail around the world and stick a flag in. 'I claim India for Britain!' And they're going, 'You can't claim us, we live here! Five hundred million of us!' 'Do you have a flag? ... No flag, no country! Those are the rules, that...I just made up.'

There was a spirit of ex-empire, this thing of 'things can't be done', whereas in America, I thought there was a spirit of 'can be done!', the pioneer thing. 'Go do it, what do you want to do?' 'I want to put babies on spikes.' 'Go, then! Go! What a wonderful idea. It's the American Dream!'

'Danger' could be my middle name … but it's 'John'.

Cats have a scam going – you buy the food, they eat the food, they go away; that's the deal.

We throw sticks at dogs, that's the level we have dogs at. You'd never dream of throwing one for a cat. We throw sticks for dogs, and dogs go, 'Oh, he's dropped his stick! I better go and get that... (mimes chasing after the stick) Saw you dropped your stick there. Thought I'd bring it back... And you hang on... (mimes giving the stick back and follows it with eyes as it's thrown again) Did you see me just bring that back? And then you...you dropped it again? This is very weird I don't know what's going on here (mimes bringing the stick back again) Now hang on to it this time, I don't want to piss about all the time. You think I enjoy this? There you... Don't fucking throw it!!' That's why the third time, when they come back, they won't give it to you, they go, (through clenched teeth) 'No... I won't let you take it!'.

Jerry Seinfeld

Born:
April 29, 1954 in Brooklyn, New York, USA.

Career:
Seinfeld's interest in comedy is said to have started when he was eight years old. He is described as a goal-oriented performer and he started doing stand-up in New York-clubs right after he quit college. Allegedly, he performed for free, just to rehearse his stand-up comedy. His career took off 1981, after doing The Tonight Show Starring Johnny Carson. He then became a regular guest on Late Night With David Letterman and was voted Funniest Male Stand-Up Comic at the American Comedy Awards.

In 1989, Seinfeld and his college buddy Larry David got a contract with the NBC to do 'a show about nothing'. Seinfeld became one of USA's most popular TV-shows ever, and became a smash hit with both viewers and critics. Seinfeld went on for eight years and was rewarded with innumerable awards. After the final show, Jerry Seinfeld has written best-selling books, done commercial webisodes promoting American Express and he also wrote Bee Movie in 2007.

The Swiss have an interesting army. Five hundred years without a war. Pretty impressive. Also pretty lucky for them. Ever see that little Swiss Army knife they have to fight with? Not much of a weapon there. Corkscrews. Bottle openers. 'Come on, buddy, let's go. You get past me, the guy in back of me, he's got a spoon. Back off. I've got the toe clippers right here.'

Where lipstick is concerned, the important thing is not color, but to accept God's final word on where your lips end.

Dogs are the leaders of the planet. If you see two life forms, one of them's making a poop, the other one's carrying it for him, who would you assume is in charge?

Dogs have no money. Isn't that amazing? They're broke their entire lives. But they get through. You know why dogs have no money? No pockets.

I had a parakeet that used to fly around the house and crash into these huge mirrors my mother put in. Ever heard of this interior design principle, that a mirror makes it seem like you have an entire other room? What kind of jerk walks up to a mirror and goes, 'Hey look, there's a whole other room in there. There's a guy that looks just like me in there.' But the parakeet would fall for this. I'd let him out of his cage, he'd fly right into the mirror. And I'd always think, 'Even if he thinks the mirror is another room, why doesn't he at least try to avoid hitting the other parakeet?'.

I was in front of an ambulance the other day, and I noticed that the word 'ambulance' was spelled in reverse print on the hood of the ambulance. And I thought, 'Well, isn't that clever.' I look in the rear-view mirror, I can read the word 'ambulance' behind me. Of course while you're reading, you don't see where you're going, you crash, you need an ambulance. I think they're trying to drum up some business on the way back from lunch.

I was the best man at the wedding. If I'm the best man, why is she marrying him?

My parents didn't want to move to Florida, but they turned sixty and that's the law.

The suit is definitely the universal business outfit for men. There is nothing else men like to wear when doing business. I don't know why it projects this image of power. Why is it intimidating? 'We'd better do what this guy says, his pants match his jacket.'

Why do people give each other flowers? To celebrate various important occasions, they're killing living creatures? Why restrict it to plants? 'Sweetheart, let's make up. Have this deceased squirrel.'

Why do they call it a 'building'? It looks like they're finished. Why isn't it a 'built'?

Would somebody please explain to me those signs that say, 'No animals allowed except for Seeing Eye Dogs?' Who is that sign for? Is it for the dog, or the blind person?

A dog will stay stupid. That's why we love them so much. The entire time we know them, they're idiots. Think of your dog. Everytime you come home, he thinks it's amazing. He has no idea how you accomplish this every day. You walk in the door, the joy of this experience overwhelms him. He looks at you, 'He's back, it's that guy, that same guy.' He can't believe it. Everything is amazing to your dog. 'Another can of food? I don't believe it.'

You can measure distance by time. 'How far away is it? Oh about 20 minutes.' But it doesn't work the other way. 'When do you get off work? Around 3 miles.'

The government is basically parents for adults.

Men want the same thing from their underwear that they want from women: a little bit of support, and a little bit of freedom.

Henry Youngman

Born:
March 16, 1906, in Whitechapel, London, UK.

Died:
February 24, 1998, New York, New York, USA.

Career:
Youngman started his career as an orchestra musician. During the band's performances, Youngman often entertained the audience with jokes. One night, the regular comedian didn't show for his performance. Youngman filled his spot and that started his stand-up career. He started touring diligently and his big break-through came in 1937, performing at a popular radio show. Henry Youngman made numerous appearances in television and kept touring.

Youngman never retired, and he performed his stage act until his final days.

I'll tell you how to beat the gambling in Las Vegas. When you get off the airplane, walk right into the propeller.

My wife and I have the secret to making a marriage last. Two times a week, we go to a nice restaurant, a little wine, good food..... She goes Tuesdays, I go Fridays.

She was at the beauty shop for two hours. That was only for the estimate. She got a mudpack and looked great for two days. Then the mud fell off.

There was a girl knocking on my hotel room door all night! Finally, I let her out.

My Grandmother is over eighty and still doesn't need glasses. Drinks right out of the bottle.

Jay Leno

Born:
April 28, 1950, in New Rochelle, New York, USA.

Career:
Jay Leno started his career touring and performing at clubs in the US. Leno distinguished himself as a busy bee, with about 300 acts every year. The touring paid off: he became very popular, with a large audience.

In the middle of the 1980's, Leno started taking part on late night TV. He made numerous appearances, among others at Late Night with David Letterman and at The Tonight Show starring Johnny Carson.

When Carson quit in 1992, Leno took over the hosting assignment on the Tonight Show. They then changed the name of the show to The Tonight Show with Jay Leno. In 1995, Leno won an Emmy for hosting The Tonight Show.

Leno has appeared as himself in many feature films including Dave (1993), Mad City (1997), Space Cowboys (2000) and Mr. 3000 (2004).

I've never understood why women love cats. Cats are independent, they don't listen, they don't come in when you call, they like to stay out all night, and when they're home they like to be left alone and sleep. In other words, every quality that women hate in a man, they love in a cat.

If God had wanted us to vote, he would have given us candidates.

An Israeli man's life was saved when he was given a Palestinian man's heart in a heart transplant operation. The guy is doing fine, but the bad news is, he can't stop throwing rocks at himself.

I went into a McDonald's yesterday and said, 'I'd like some fries.' The girl at the counter said, 'Would you like some fries with that?'

Go through your phone book, call people and ask them to drive you to the airport. The ones who will drive you are your true friends. The rest aren't bad people; they're just acquaintances.

Now there are more overweight people in America than average-weight people. So overweight people are now average. Which means you've met your New Year's resolution.

According to a new survey, women say they feel more comfortable undressing in front of men than they do undressing in front of other women. They say that women are too judgmental, where, of course, men are just grateful.

Penthouse offered Lewinsky $2 million to pose nude. This confirms what Clinton said in his State of the Union address - he is creating high paying jobs for young people.

Conan O'Brien

Born:
April 18, 1963 in Brookline, Massachusetts, USA.

Career:
Conan went to Harvard, majoring in history and literature and also became the president of the Harvard humor magazine; the Harvard Lampoon. After finishing studies at Harvard, O'Brien went for his career as a comedian. He started with a television writing job at HBO's Not Necessarily the News in Los Angeles. He spent two years with that show. In 1988, O'Brien moved to New York to start working with Saturday Night Live and one year later he won an Emmy for 'Outstanding Writing in a Comedy or Variety Series'. He left Saturday Night Live in 1991 to work as a scriptwriter and producer for the Simpsons.

He started hosting his own show in 1993, Late Night with Conan O'Brien. O'Brien has been voted one of the '50 Funniest People Alive' by Entertainment Weekly magazine.

A study in the Washington Post says that women have better verbal skills than men. I just want to say to the authors of that study: Duh.

CBS news anchor Dan Rather has interviewed Iraqi dictator Saddam Hussein. When asked what it was like to talk to a crazy man, Saddam said, 'It's not so bad.'

Scientists announced that they have located the gene for alcoholism. Scientists say they found it at a party, talking way too loudly.

Rita Rudner

Born:
September 17, 1956, in Miami, Florida, USA.

Career:
Rita Rudner is one of the most famous female stand-up comedians. Rudner started working in show business as a fifteen-year-old dancer on Broadway. Six years after her Broadway-premiere, she started doing stand-up in clubs. Her TV-debut came in 1985 as a comedian at the 9th Annual Young Comedians Special at HBO which Rodney Dangerfield hosted. A few years touring in the US followed after that.

By 1989, she had landed her first solo gig on HBO with One Night Stand: Rita Rudner. She's also been on The Tonight Show Starring Johnny Carson and Comic Relief.

Rita Rudner is also a scriptwriter and an author. Rudner has received a bunch of awards. In 1990, she won the American Comedy Award as Best Female Stand-up.

When I was a kid, I had two friends, and they were imaginary and they would only play with each other.

Some women hold up dresses that are so ugly and they always say the same thing: 'This looks much better on.' On what? On fire?

I want to have children, but my friends scare me. One of my friends told me she was in labor for 36 hours. I don't even want to do anything that feels good for 36 hours.

My husband and I are either going to buy a dog or have a child. We can't decide to ruin our carpet or ruin our lives.

Before I met my husband I'd never fallen in love, though I've stepped in it a few times.

I love being married. It's so great to find that one special person you want to annoy for the rest of your life.

A man will go to war, fight and die for his country. But he won't get a bikini wax.

I think men who have a pierced ear are better prepared for marriage. They've experienced pain and bought jewelry.

Marriages don't last. When I meet a guy, the first question I ask myself is: is this the man I want my children to spend their weekends with?

The word 'aerobics' came about when the gym instructors got together and said: If we're going to charge $10 an hour, we can't call it Jumping up and down.

Paula Poundstone

Born:
December 29, 1959, in Huntsville, Alabama, USA.

Career:
Poundstone attended Lincoln-Sudbury Regional High School. Eventually she dropped out to pursue a show business career. But Poundstone chose comedy instead and started doing stand-up comedy on open-mike nights in Boston in 1979. She later moved to California to continue her career. She began appearing on several talk shows.

In 1989, she won the American Comedy Award for 'Best Female Stand-Up Comic.' In 1990, she wrote and starred in an HBO special; Cats, Cops and Stuff and subsequently won a CableACE Award for the show. In 1993, Poundstone won a second CableACE Award.

Poundstone is number 88 on Comedy Central's list of the 100 greatest stand-ups of all time.

My mom said she learned how to swim when someone took her out in the lake and threw her off the boat. I said, 'Mom, they weren't trying to teach you how to swim.'

I was born in Alabama, but I only lived there for a month before I'd done everything there was to do.

Adults are always asking little kids what they want to be when they grow up because they're looking for ideas.

The problem with cats is that they get the same exact look whether they see a moth or an ax-murderer.

Can you remember when you didn't want to sleep? Isn't it inconceivable? I guess the definition of adulthood is that you want to sleep.

We need a twelve-step group for compulsive talkers. They would call it On Anon Anon.

Larry Miller

Born:
October 15, 1953, in Valley Stream, New York, USA.

Career:
Miller began his career playing piano and drums in New York City bars. He switched to comedy and quickly became successful. He started performing in clubs all over the US after only two years. In the late 1980's, he began making movies and he has starred in films such as Out Cold, Three Fugitives and Pretty Woman.

In 1992, Miller starred in his own HBO comedy special, Larry Miller: Just Words, which was nominated for a CableACE Award. He has regular guest appearances on The Tonight Show and Late Night with David Letterman.

I just broke up with someone and the last thing she said to me was, 'You'll never find anyone like me again!' I'm thinking, 'I should hope not! If I don't want you, why would I want someone like you?'

Women say they have sexual thoughts too. They have no idea. It's the difference between shooting a bullet and throwing it. If they knew what we were really thinking, they'd never stop slapping us.

Steven Wright

Born:
December 6, 1955 in New York, New York, USA.

Career:
Wright began his stand-up career in the late 1970's, performing in Boston comedy clubs. In 1982, he made his first appearance on The Tonight Show starring Johnny Carson. In 1985, he released his debut comedy album I Have a Pony, which was nominated for a Grammy Award.

During the 1980's he also guest hosted Saturday Night Live. Wright is also an actor and in 1989, Steven Wright was awarded an academy award for writing and starring in the short film The Appointments of Dennis Jennings. Other films Wright starred in are Natural Born Killers and Desperately Seeking Susan.

If God dropped acid, would he see people?

I busted a mirror and got seven years bad luck.
But my lawyer thinks he can get me five.

I was once walking through the forest, alone, and a tree fell
right in front of me, and I didn't hear it.

I was sad because I had no shoes, until I met a man who had
no feet. So I said, 'Got any shoes you're not using?'

I took a course in speed waiting. Now I can wait an hour in
only ten minutes.

I went to the hardware store and bought some used paint. It
was in the shape of a house. I also bought some batteries,
but they weren't included... So I had to buy 'em again.

My mechanic told me, 'I couldn't repair your brakes, so I made your horn louder.'

OK, so what's the speed of dark?

Shin: a device for finding furniture in the dark.

I used to have an open mind but my brains kept falling out.

If you can't hear me, it's because I'm in parentheses.

Right now I'm having amnesia and déjà-vu at the same time. I think I've forgotten this before.

I stayed up all night playing poker with tarot cards. I got a full house and four people died.

You can't have everything. Where would you put it?

A lot of people are afraid of heights.
Not me; I'm afraid of widths.

When I turned two I was really anxious, because I'd doubled my age in a year. I thought, 'If this keeps up, by the time I'm six I'll be ninety.'

When I get real bored, I like to drive downtown and get a great parking spot, then sit in my car and count how many people ask me if I'm leaving.

I bought my brother some gift-wrap for Christmas. I took it to the Gift Wrap department and told them to wrap it, but in a different print so he would know when to stop unwrapping.

There was a power outage at a department store yesterday. Twenty people were trapped on the escalators.

I have a hobby. I have the world's largest collection of sea shells. I keep it scattered on beaches all over the world. Maybe you've seen it.

I can remember the first time I had to go to sleep. Mom said, 'Steven, time to go to sleep.' I said, 'But I don't know how.' She said, 'It's real easy. Just go down to the end of tired and hang a left.' So I went down to the end of tired, and just out of curiosity I hung a right. My mother was there, and she said 'I thought I told you to go to sleep.'

Emo Philips

Born:
February 7 1956, Chicago, Illinois, USA.

Career:
Philips started his career performing in various Chicago comedy clubs in the beginning of the 1980's. His big break came in 1984 when he made his first appearance on Late Night with David Letterman. That same year he released his first comedy album: E=MO Squared.

Philips has also had acting roles on television shows such as Miami Vice and the "Weird Al" Yankovic Show.

Philips was also included in the top 50 of E4's 100 Greatest Comedians and he has won several awards. Jay Leno once described him as the best joke writer in America.

And always remember the last words of my grandfather, who said, 'A truck!'

How many people here have telekenetic powers?
Raise my hand.

I love to go down to the schoolyard and watch all the little children jump up and down and run around yelling and screaming. They don't know I'm only using blanks.

I was walking down fifth avenue today and I found a wallet, and I was gonna keep it, rather than return it, but I thought: well, if I lost a hundred and fifty dollars, how would I feel? And I realized I would want to be taught a lesson.

Probably the toughest time in anyone's life is when you have to murder a loved one because they're the devil.

The way I understand it, the Russians are sort of a combination of evil and incompetence... sort of like the Post Office with tanks.

Whatever happened to the good ole days, when children worked in factories?

You don't appreciate a lot of stuff in school until you get older. Little things like being spanked every day by a middle-aged woman: Stuff you pay good money for in later life.

I read somewhere that 77 per cent of all the mentally ill live in poverty. Actually, I'm more intrigued by the 23 per cent who are apparently doing quite well for themselves.

Bill Cosby

Born:
July 12, 1937, in Philadelphia, Pennsylvania, USA.

Career:
After working as a bartender for several years, Cosby began his career as a stand-up comic. He appeared on various shows, including The Ed Sullivan Show. His big break came in 1965 when he appeared as Alexander Scott in I Spy (1965). It was the first time an African-American actor starred in a weekly dramatic television series.

Cosby kept doing films during the 1970's, while he was studying. He received a doctorate in education from the University of Massachusetts.

In 1984, he started the sitcom; The Cosby show. During the 1980's, Cosby was among the highest paid entertainers in USA. The TV-show aired until 1994 and received numerous awards.

I haven't slept for ten days, because that would be too long.

I would imagine if you understood Morse Code, a tap dancer would drive you crazy.

I played golf....I did not get a hole in one, but I did hit a guy and that's way more satisfying. Your supposed to yell FORE, but I was too busy mumbling 'that ain't no way that's gonna hit him.'

I bought a doughnut and they gave me a receipt for the doughnut... I don't need a receipt for the doughnut. I give you money and you give me the doughnut, end of transaction. We don't need to bring ink and paper into this. I can't imagine a scenario that I would have to prove that I bought a doughnut. To some skeptical friend, 'Don't even act like I didn't buy a doughnut, I've got the documentation right here... It's in my file at home. ...Under D.'

When someone hands you a flyer, it's like they're saying 'here you throw this away.'

I like rice. Rice is great if your hungry and want 2000 of something.

I don't own a cell phone or a pager. I just hang around everyone I know, all the time. If someone wants to get a hold of me they just say 'Mitch,' and I say 'What?' and turn my head slightly.

I was at the airport and this guy came up to me and said I saw you on tv last night. He didn't say if I was any good. He just told me where I was. So I turned away for a minute and said 'Hey I saw you at the airport a minute ago. You were good.'

One time a guy handed me a picture of himself and he said. 'Here's a picture of me when I was younger.' Every picture of you is when you were younger. Here's a picture of me when I'm older. How'd you pull that off? Let me see that camera.

I went to the airport, I put my bag in the x-ray machine, I found out my bag has cancer. It only has six more months to hold stuff.

This one commercial said, 'Forget everything you know about slipcovers.' So I did, and it was a load off of my mind. Then the commercial tried to sell slipcovers, but I didn't know what they were!

You know when you see an advertisement for a casino, and they have a picture of a guy winning money? That's false advertising, because that happens the least. That's like if you're advertising a hamburger, they could show a guy choking. 'This is what happened once.'

I saw a seagull hanging out by a lake, but I said, 'Don't worry, Dude. I won't say anything.'

I was going to stay overnight at my friend's house - he said, 'You'll have to sleep on the floor.' Damn gravity! You don't know how bad I wanted to sleep on the wall.

I was in a convenience store, reading a magazine. The clerk told me, 'This is not a library!' 'OK! I will talk louder, then!'

Lenny Bruce

Born:
October 13, 1925, in Mineola, Long Island, New York, USA.

Died:
August 3, 1966, Hollywood, California, USA.

Career:
Lenny Bruce was a controversial American stand-up comedian and satirist of the 1950's and 1960's. He started his career by performing in small nightclubs. In 1948, he did the Arthur Godfrey's Talent Scouts TV-show, and slowly, his audience grew bigger and bigger. His comedy was controversial though, and in 1961, he was arrested on obscenity charges following an appearance at the Jazz Workshop in San Francisco. Several religious groups also tried to stop his tabu-comedy and in 1964, he was arrested again.

Bruce was a very popular comedian, but in 1965, he was broke and in debt. On August 3, 1966, Lenny was found on the bathroom floor of his Hollywood home, dead from a drug overdose at the age of 40.

In 2004, Bruce was voted No. 3 of the 100 Greatest Stand-ups of All Time by Comedy Central.

If Jesus had been killed 20 years ago, Catholic school children would be wearing little Electric Chairs around their necks instead of crosses.

Miami Beach is where neon goes to die.

I won't say ours was a tough school, but we had our own coroner. We used to write essays like: What I'm going to be if I grow up.

Never tell. Not if you love your wife... In fact, if your old lady walks in on you, deny it. Yeah. Just flat out and she'll believe it: 'I'm tellin' ya. This chick came downstairs with a sign around her neck 'Lay on Top of Me Or I'll Die.' I didn't know what I was gonna do....'

I sort of felt sorry for the damn flies. They never hurt anybody. Even though they were supposed to carry diseases I never heard of anybody saying they caught something from a fly. My cousin gave two guys the clap and nobody ever whacked her with a paper.

Elayne Boosler

Born:
August 18, 1952 in New York City, New York, USA.

Career:
Elayne Boosler was a waitress at a comedy club in Brooklyn. Andy Kaufman played there, and he convinced her she should go onstage. Boosler was an instant success and started her career by touring clubs and college campuses. Her first television appearance was on the Tonight Show with guest host Helen Reddy.

When Boosler became known, the field was then still dominated by male performers. In 1986, Boosler became the first female to get her own comedy special on cable when Showtime aired Party of One.

To date, Boosler has done seven cable specials and she has also made it as an actress.

I know what men want. Men want to be really, really close to someone who will leave them alone.

My ancestors wandered lost in the wilderness for forty years because even in biblical times, men would not stop to ask for directions.

The Vatican is against surrogate mothers. Good thing they didn't have that rule when Jesus was born.

I have six locks on my door all in a row. When I go out, I lock every other one. I figure no matter how long somebody stands there picking the locks, they are always locking three.

You never see a man walking down the street with a woman who has a little potbelly and a bald spot.

We have women in the military, but they don't put us in the front lines. They don't know if we can fight, if we can kill. I think we can. All the general has to do is walk over to the women and say, 'You see the enemy over there? They say you look fat in those uniforms.'

Drew Carey

Born:
May 23, 1958, in Cleveland, Ohio, USA.

Career:
Carey joined the Marine Corps reserves in the 1980's. In 1985, he began his comedy career and for the next few years he performed at comedy clubs in Cleveland and Los Angeles. In 1988, he competed in Star Search and that's when he became famous to the larger TV-audience. In 1991, he did the Tonight Show Starring Johnny Carson and Late Night with David Letterman. In 1995, Carey got his own stand-up sitcom; the self-titled television show the Drew Carey Show, which aired up until 2004.

Carey has won awards such as the CableACE Award for Best Writing for the Drew Carey Show. Carey is also the author of the book Dirty Jokes and Beer: Stories of the Unrefined.

I'm not a good lover, but at least I'm fast.

Hate your job? There's a support group for that.
It's called everybody and they meet at a bar.

Someone once said that there'd be no wars if women ran
the world..... well that's a load of crap.. I'm sure that no one
would start a fight for no reason if women ran the world...

You know that look women get when they want sex?
Me neither.

It isn`t premarital sex if you have no intention of getting
married.

I always get screwed by the system. That's my place in the
universe. I'm the system's bitch.

Steve Martin

Born:
August 14, 1945, in Waco, Texas, USA.

Career:
Steve Martin dropped out of college at age 21 to start a career in comedy. His career took off quickly and he toured and performed at different comedy clubs. After having performed at Saturday Night Live and The Tonight Show Starring Johnny Carson, Steve Martin became known to every American. During the 1970's, Steve Martin was the most successful stand-up comedian in the US.

During the 1980's, Martin began making comedies like Parenthood (1989), Father of the Bride (1991), LA Story (1991) and Bowfinger (1999).

In the year 2000, Steve Martin received a Lifetime Achievement Award in Comedy.

A day without sunshine is like, you know, night.

Boy, those French: they have a different word for everything!

Don't have sex man. It leads to kissing and pretty soon you have to start talking to them.

First the doctor told me the good news: I was going to have a disease named after me.

I believe that sex is one of the most beautiful, natural, wholesome things that money can buy.

I like a woman with a head on her shoulders. I hate necks.

There is one thing I would break up over, and that is if she caught me with another woman. I won't stand for that.

Talking about music is like dancing about architecture.

I believe in eight of the ten commandments; and I believe in going to church every Sunday unless there's a game on.

All I've ever wanted was an honest week's pay for an honest day's work.

I saw the movie, 'Crouching Tiger, Hidden Dragon' and I was surprised because I didn't see any tigers or dragons. And then I realised why: they're crouching and hidden.

A celebrity is anyone who looks like he spends more than two hours working on his hair.

I used to smoke marijuana. But I'll tell you something: I would only smoke it in the late evening. Oh, occasionally the early evening, but usually the late evening - or the mid-evening. Just the early evening, midevening and late evening. Occasionally, early afternoon, early midafternoon, or perhaps the late-midafternoon. Oh, sometimes the early-mid-late-early morning. . . But never at dusk.

Ellen DeGeneres

Born:
January 26, 1958 in Metairie, Louisiana, USA.

Career:
After graduating high school, DeGeneres worked a variety of jobs in New Orleans. In 1981, she did her stand-up debut at an area coffee house's amateur. Just one year after that, she won a "Funniest Person in America" competion sponsored by the Showtime cable network. This win made DeGeneres move to San Francisco to pursue her comedy career. In 1986, she performed at The Tonight Show with Johnny Carson.

Ellen's comedy material was turned into the successful sit-com Ellen in 1994. The series aired up until 1998 and DeGeneres made history for her portrayal of TV's first openly gay lead character sitcom.

In 2003, she got her own talk show: The Ellen DeGeneres Show. The show has earned multiple Daytime Emmy Awards for Best Talk Show and Best Talk Show Host.

I ask people why they have deer heads on their walls. They always say because it's such a beautiful animal. There you go. I think my mother is attractive, but I have photographs of her.

In the beginning there was nothing. God said, Let there be light! And there was light. There was still nothing, but you could see it a whole lot better.

The 1960s were when hallucinogenic drugs were really, really big. And I don't think it's a coincidence that we had the shows then like The Flying Nun.

I remember one day I was coming home from kindergarten, well, I thought it was kindergarten, it turned out later I'd been working in a factory for two years... I was wondering 'cause it was always really hot and everyone was older than me, but, um, what did I know?

I have a terrible problem with procrastination... a friend told me, 'Well, you should go to therapy.' And I thought about it, but then I said, 'Wait a minute. Why should I pay a stranger to listen to me talk when I can get strangers to pay to listen to me talk?' And that's when I got the idea of touring.

My grandmother started walking five miles a day when she was sixty. She's ninety-seven now, and we don't know where the hell she is.

I gotta work out. I keep saying it all the time. I keep saying I gotta start working out. It's been about two months since I've worked out. And I just don't have the time. Which uh..is odd. Because I have the time to go out to dinner. And uh..and watch tv. And get a bone density test. And uh.. try to figure out what my phone number spells in words.

Just go up to somebody on the street and say 'You're it!' and just run away.

Normal is getting dressed in clothes that you buy for work and driving through traffic in a car that you are still paying for - in order to get to the job you need to pay for the clothes and the car, and the house you leave vacant all day so you can afford to live in it.

I was raised around heterosexuals, as all heterosexuals are, that's where us gay people come from... you heterosexuals.

Let's say, for instance, I'm out of cheese. And then I'll think, oh, but what if I go to the store and they're out of cheese? I'd be like, 'How can you be out of cheese? What do you mean? How can we be out of cheese? You're out of cheese. People run out of cheese.' Then I'd be like, 'Yeah, but you're a store. You should have cheese stocked up in the back for people like me coming in looking for cheese.' And that's when they send the manager over, who thinks he's so cool for being the manager 'cause his picture's framed in the front of the store 'cause he's the manager, you know. And he'd be like, 'What seems to be the problem, ma'am?' Which to me is so condescending, like 'little lady.' I'd be like, 'The little lady's problem....' He'd be like, 'Who's the little lady?' I'd be like, 'Shut up and listen to me. You're out of cheese and I want some.' And, he's like, 'Well, how about some cottage cheese?' Like he's going to negotiate the situation, he's a diplomat because he's the manager. And I'd be like, 'I don't want cottage cheese; I want cheddar cheese. Sharp cheddar cheese is what I came in for. Sharp cheddar cheese and cottage cheese are not the same things. Just 'cause they have the name cheese in the title doesn't make it a cheese at all. That'd be like going into a musical instrument store and saying 'I'd like to buy a trumpet,' and them saying 'I'm sorry, we're all out of trumpets, but would you like a shoe-horn?' See, that's not the same thing, is it, Mr. Manager?' And he starts getting all nervous and everything, because a crowd has formed and he starts feeling humiliated because they're all sitting around mumbling 'What seems to be the problem?

I don't know, she wants some cheese.' And, so, um, he just slaps me right across the face. And, umm, so that's when Skip, the part time guy who works there, who hates the manager 'cause he thinks so cool for being the manager and treats Skip like shit because he's just the part time guy. And Skip's going to quit in the fall and go back to school anyway. He doesn't even need the money; he's from a wealthy family. He's just doing it for the experience because his family wants him to work one summer. And, so anyway, so, he takes the hose, and he goes to spray the manager right in the eye, right, and so, but that's when he's leaning down to pick the cottage cheese, so he misses him and he gets this old woman who's standing right behind him, and she's there picking out an avocado, because the older you are the less you eat and she all she wants is the avocado. So she screams out, 'My eye, I've been sprayed in the eye with a produce hose.' And so then that's when her nephew who's visiting from Austin, Texas is two aisles over buying tortilla chips because he thinks they're going to have guacamole. Little does he know it's one avocado. And so, he starts running 'I'll help you, aunt so and so,' running, and then when he's running down the aisle when he slips on some water from the produce hose, breaks his leg, breaks his arm, bruises two ribs right there… gets a stitch put in his cheekbone, just one, but still, it's a stitch. Chaos breaks out and it's all over Hard Copy and Entertainment Tonight and Access Hollywood… 'Lesbian Demands Cheese, Causes Riot.' And I'm like, 'I didn't even want the cheese.' You know?

Phyllis Diller

Born:
July 17, 1917 in Lima, Ohio, USA.

Diller was a housewife, mother and advertising copywriter when she started her career playing comedy clubs in the San Francisco Bay area. She became known to the larger audience as a contestant on Groucho Marx's quiz show You Bet Your Life. That made her extremely popular everywhere in the US. She sold out for 87 straight weeks at San Francisco legendary Purple Onion nightclub. That was followed by endless appearances on TV specials, such as The Ed Sullivan Show and every Bob Hope Christmas Special from 1965 through 1994. Diller is also an actress and has done numerous films.

In 1992, Diller received a Lifetime Achievement Award in Comedy, and since the 1950's, she's got a record in the Guinness Book of World Records for delivering 12 punch lines per minute!

If it weren't for baseball, many kids wouldn't know what a millionaire looks like.

A bachelor is a guy who never made the same mistake once.

Cleaning your house while your kids are still growing is like shoveling the sidewalk before it stops snowing.

I asked the waiter, 'Is this milk fresh?' He said, 'Lady, three hours ago it was grass.'

We spend the first twelve months of our children's lives teaching them to walk and talk and the next twelve telling them to sit down and shut up.

What I don't like about office Christmas parties is looking for a job the next day.

Peter Kay

Born:
June 2, 1973, in Farnworth, Bolton, England.

Career:
Peter Kay was born and brought up in Bolton, UK. After leaving school, he worked his way through several part time jobs. These included working in a factory, a warehouse, a petrol station and a Bingo hall.

His big break came when he auditioned for the North West Comedian of the Year competition in 1996 and was voted best act. This launched his stand-up career. In 1997, he also won Channel 4's So You Think You're Funny contest and is today one of Britain's top comedians.

Kay did TV-shows such as the Peter Kay thing and Phoenix Nights. In the UK, his most famous act; Mum Wants a Bungalow, won in a 100 Greatest Funny Moments-vote. In 2003, he was listed in The Observer as one of the 50 Funniest British Comedians.

When I was a kid I used to pray every night for a new bike. Then I realized that The Lord doesn't work that way, so I stole one and asked him to forgive me.

I've often wanted to drown my troubles, but I can't get my wife to go swimming.

I went to a restaurant that serves 'breakfast at any time'. So I ordered French Toast during the Renaissance.

If we aren't supposed to eat animals, then why are they made out of meat?

I think animal testing is a terrible idea; they get all nervous and give the wrong answers.

So I was having dinner with Garry Kasporov and there was a check tablecloth. It took him two hours to pass me the salt.

Billy Connolly

Born:
November 24, 1942, in Anderston, Glasgow, Scotland.

Career:
Connolly's career started by coincidence, he was an accomplished banjo player and a member of the band Humblebums with Gerry Rafferty. The jokes he told between songs eventually took over his act. That's why Connolly chose to go for a career in comedy instead. After quitting the music industry to pursue comedy, he did a lot of touring. He became famous in the UK in the beginning of the 1970's after appearing on Parkinson. In 1979, Connolly made his film debut in Absolution.

In the late 1980s, he also periodically performed at Saturday Night Live and David Letterman. He also did an HBO special with Whoopie Goldberg.

The human race has been set up. Someone, somewhere, is playing a practical joke on us. Apparently, women need to feel loved to have sex. Men need to have sex to feel loved. How do we ever get started?

I worry about ridiculous things, you know, how does a guy who drives a snowplough get to work in the morning. . . . That can keep me awake for days...

I don't believe in angels and I have trouble with the whole God thing. I don't want to say I don't believe in God, but I don't think I do. But I believe in people who do.

If Jesus was a Jew, how come he has a Mexican first name?

Two guys are talking and one says to the other: 'What would you do if the end of the world was in 3 minutes time?' The other one says, 'I'd sh*g everything that moved...What would you do?' And he says, 'I'd stand perfectly still.'

Save the Trees?...Trees are the main cause of Forest Fires!

What is it with McDonald's staff who pretend they don't understand you unless you insert the 'Mc' before the item you're ordering? It has to be a McChicken burger...a chicken burger gets blank looks. Well, I'll have a McStraw and jam it into your McEyes, you f**cking McTosser!

I don't know why I should have to learn Algebra... I'm never likely to go there.

RICHARD PRYOR

Born:
December 1, 1940, in Peoria, Illinois, USA.

Died:
December 10th, 2005.

Career:
Richard Pryor had a rough childhood and was raised in his grandmother's brothel. He had several jobs when he was young, including truck driver, meat packer and he also spent a few years in the US Army. After he left the services in 1960, Pryor started singing in small clubs. Shortly after, he pursued a comedy-career instead, and also got minor roles in The Busy Body (1967) and Wild in the Street (1968).

Pryor did several live specials, such as the dynamic Richard Pryor (1971), Live in Concert (1979), Richard Pryor Live on Sunset Strip (1982) and Richard Pryor... Here and Now (1983).

In 1993, he was rewarded a Lifetime Achievement Award in comedy and he has also received several Grammy's.

He was married a total of seven times, and fathered eight children. After long battles with ill health, Richard Pryor passed away on December 10th, 2005.

Let me tell you what really happened... Every night before I go to bed, I have milk and cookies. One night I mixed some low-fat milk and some pasteurized, then I dipped my cookie in and the shit blew up.

I went through every phone book in Africa, and I didn't find one god damned Pryor!

I'd like to die like my father died... My father died fucking. My father was 57 when he died. The woman was 18. My father came and went at the same time.

Bitch was so fine I'd suck her daddy's dick.

I believe in the institution of marriage, and I intend to keep trying 'til I get it right.

I never met anybody who said when they were a kid, 'I wanna grow up and be a critic.'

I'm not addicted to cocaine... I just like the way it smells.

'White people go; Why you guys hold your things (penis)? Cause you done took every thing else motherfucka!'

I had to stop drinkin, cuz I got tired of waking in my car driving ninety.

What I never understand about a hangover is, where does the breath come from. You know what I mean? I mean, is someone shitting in your mouth?

And its the people you meet after you been drunk, that remember shit you don't remember.. ..'Hey Rich, don't you remember that time we went out, we got fucked up, and you stuck your arm up that elephant's ass? Don't you remember that? Elephant tightened his ass up and went walking down the street with you? Don't you remember that? Man, you looked like a turd with a hat on.'

If you want some pussy, you'll talk all that shit with them. 'Hey, yeah, sure, the cosmos.. sure..'

Lily Tomlin

Born:
September 1, 1939, in Detroit, Michigan, USA.

Career:
After college, Tomlin began doing stand-up comedy in night-clubs in Detroit and then New York City. Her first television appearance was on The Merv Griffin Show in 1965 and Tomlin joined the Laugh-In cast in 1969.

Tomlin starred in six comedy television specials: The Lily Tomlin Show (1973), Lily (1973), Lily (1974), Lily Tomlin (1975), Lily: SoldOut (1981), and Lily for President? (1982), In the 1990's, Tomlin appeared as a regular on the popular sitcom Murphy Brown.

Tomlin has garnered several Tony Awards and Emmy Awards, as well as a Grammy Award. In 2003 she won the Mark Twain Prize for American Humor.

I always wanted to be somebody, but now I realize I should have been more specific.

The problem with winning the rat race is you're still a rat.

There's so much plastic in this culture that vinyl leopard skin is becoming an endangered synthetic.

We have reason to believe that man first walked upright to free his hands for masturbation.

Things are going to get a lot worse before they get worse.

Why is it that when we talk to God we're said to be praying, but when God talks to us we're schizophrenic?

I worry that the person who thought up Muzak may be thinking up something else.

Bill Hicks

Born:
December 16, 1961, in Valdosta, Georgia, USA.

Died:
February 26, 1994.

Career:
Hicks was drawn to comedy at an early age, and is said to have been given permission by one of his teachers to tell jokes to his classmates at school.

He started in 1978, despite the fact that he was too young, performing at the Comedy Workshop. He moved to Los Angeles after graduation and started performing at the Comedy Store in Hollywood.

In 1984, he did Late Night with David Letterman, and ended up doing eleven more appearances. In 1990, he released his first album, Dangerous, performed on the HBO special One Night Stand and during the 1990's, he just kept touring. By the early 1990's, he hit it big time, even though his reputation suffered from drug use.

He died from pancreatic cancer on February 26, 1994, at the age of 32.

People are bringing shotguns to UFO sightings in Fife, Alabama. I asked a guy, 'Why do you bring a gun to a UFO sighting?' Guy said, 'Way-ul, we didn' wanna be ab-duc-ted.' If I lived in Fife, Alabama, I would be on my hands and knees every night praying for abduction.

Children are smarter than any of us. Know how I know that? I don't know one child with a full time job and children.

Childbirth is no more a miracle then eating food and a turd coming out of your ass.

Isn't that the weirdest fucking question you've ever heard? Not what am I reading, but what am I reading *for*? Well, godammit, ya stumped me! Why do I read? Well... hmmm... I dunno... I guess I read for a lot of reasons, and the main one is so I don't end up being a fucking waffle waitress.

I can speak for every guy in this room here tonight. Guys, if you could blow yourselves, ladies, you'd be in this room alone right now. Watching an empty stage.

One of my big fears in life is that I'm gonna die and my parents are going to come to clean out my apartment and find that porno wing I've been adding on to for years.

It's great to be here. I thank you. Ah, I've been on the road doing comedy for ten years now, so bear with me while I plaster on a fake smile and plough through this shit one more time.

I'm tired of this back-slapping 'Isn't humanity neat?' bullshit. We're a virus with shoes, okay? That's all we are.

The worst kind of non-smokers are the ones that come up to you and cough. That's pretty fucking cruel isn't it? Do you go up to cripples and dance too?

Robin Williams

Born:
July 21, 1951, in Chicago, Illinois, USA.

Career:
Williams studied to be a dramatic actor, first at Marin College in California and then at Juilliard. After leaving the prestigious art school, he returned to California to perform stand-up. Williams first achieved notice for his stand-up routines, and working clubs like The Purple Onion in San Francisco. His break came after an appearance in L.A.'s Comedy Store, and then he became known to American audiences as the zany alien Mork in the television comedy series Mork and Mindy.

His stand-up comedy began to reach a wider audience with three HBO comedy specials Off The Wall (1978), An Evening with Robin Williams (1982), and Robin Williams: Live at the Met (1986).

At this point, Williams was also an established actor, he did films such as Good Morning, Vietnam (1987), Dead Poets Society (1989), The Fisher King (1991) and Mrs. Doubtfire (1993).

Williams has kept doing stand-up throughout his whole career. In 2002, he did a one-man show: Robin Williams Live on Broadway. He was voted 13th on Comedy Central's list 100 Greatest Stand-ups of All Time.

Cocaine is God's way of telling you you're making too much money.

Divorce, from the Latin word meaning to rip out a man's genitals through his wallet.

God gave men both a penis and a brain, but unfortunately not enough blood supply to run both at the same time.

Never pick a fight with ugly people – they've got nothing to lose.

We had gay burglars the other night. They broke in and rearranged the furniture.

I'm sorry, if you were right, I'd agree with you.

Reality is just a crutch for people who can't cope with drugs.

Do you think God gets stoned? I think so . . . look at the platypus.

Dana Carvey

Born:
June 2, 1955, in Missoula, Montana, USA.

Career:
Carvey began his career performing stand-up around the San Francisco Bay area. In 1981, he moved to L.A. to work as an actor. He joined the Saturday Night Live ensemble in 1986. He did a sketch on Saturday Night Live, which he and Mike Myers later developed and turned into the film Wayne's World (1992) and the sequel Wayne's World 2 (1993).

Carvey returned to TV-series in 1996 with the short-lived variety show The Dana Carvey Show on ABC. During the following years, he made several appearances on Saturday Night Live.

In 2002, he starred in the film The Master of Disguise.

I'm thirty years old, but I read at the
thirty-four-year-old level.

A long time ago there was a lot of people . . .
but that was a long time ago.

You know, sometimes you can't just take an armadillo, put it
in the barn, light it on fire and expect it to make licorice.

Dave Chappelle

Born:
August 24, 1973, in Washington, D.C, USA.

Career:
Chappelle began his comedy career at the age of 14 by performing at various comedy clubs. After quitting high school, he moved to New York City to pursue a career as a comedian.

Chappelle got his first big break on the popular Def Comedy Jam series, appearing several times in 1992. After that, he continued acting in films such as Robin Hood: Men in Tights, The Nutty Professor, Con Air, Half Baked and Screwed. He also began appearing regularly on The Late Show with David Letterman and Late Night with Conan O'Brien. Comedy Central gave Dave his own show in 2003: Chappelle's Show.

Chappell has been nominated for three Primetime Emmys.

Wow. ... That's a good question. ... Is `I don't know' an acceptable answer?

I think every group of black guys should have at least one white guy in it.

You know you must be doing something right if old people like you.

Night. Night. Keep yo butthole tight.

Remember what the Bible says: He who is without sin, cast the first rock. And I shall smoketh it.

Drugs is all around you kids. Look at that magic marker cap. What the hell you think that is, some kind of crayon? Take it off and sniff it and get high.

I'm Dave Chappelle, and I like internet porn.

Bill Bailey

Born:
February 24, 1964 in Bath, Somerset, UK.

Career:
Before Bailey became a comedian, he worked as a lounge pianist, crematorium organist and door-to-door salesman. In the early 1980's, he started doing stand-up. In 1986, Bill Bailey and Toby Longworth started a double-act; The Rubber Bishop. The duo attracted a lot of attention, and became the stepping-stone for Bailey's career. But the duo broke up, and Bailey put on a one-man show: Bill Bailey´s Cosmic Jam which was very well received.

In 1995, Bailey won a Time Out award and in 1999, he won the Best Live Stand-Up award at the British Comedy Awards.

Three blokes go into a pub. Well, I say three; could have been four or five. Could have been nine or ten, doesn't matter. Could have been fifteen, twenty - fifty. Round it up. Hundred. Let's go mad, eh - two-fifty. Tell you what, double it up - five hundred. Thousand! Oh, I've gone mad! Two thousand! Five thousand! (adopting auctioneer persona) anyone five thousand, six thou, six thousand, ten thousand! Small town in Hertfordshire goes into a pub! Fifteen thousand blokes! Alright, let's go - population of Rotterdam. The Hague. Whole of Northern Holland. Mainland U.K. Let's go all the way to the top - Europe, alright? Whole of Europe goes - I say Europe. Could be Eurasia. Not the band, obviously, that's just two of them. Alright, continents - North America! Plus South America! Plus Antartica - that's just eight blokes in a weather station. Not a good example. Alright, make it a lot simpler, all the blokes on the planet go into the pub, right? And the first bloke goes up to the bar and he says 'I'll get these in.' What an idiot.

It's not a beard, it's an animal I've trained to sit very still.

Rodney Dangerfield

Born:
November 22, 1921, in Babylon, Long Island, New York.

Died:
October 5, 2004, Los Angeles, California.

Career:
Dangerfield's birth name was Jacob Cohen. He began writing jokes at the age of 15, and started performing at age 19 under the name Jack Roy. He took his act to the road for ten years, but struggled financially. At one point he was performing as a singing waiter before giving up show business. He worked as a salesman for a long time and performed during evenings to get back in the game, now using the name Rodney Dangerfield. His comeback came when he was used as a last minute replacement for another act at The Ed Sullivan Show. His performance was very well received and he started touring across nightclubs in the 1960's. His popularity grew and he also performed at The Dean Martin Show and Saturday Night Live.

Dangerfield was also active as an actor and has starred in films such as Caddyshack (1980) and Back to School (1986).

Dangerfield has received a Grammy Award and in 1994, he won an American Comedy Award for lifetime creative achievement.

I haven't spoken to my wife in years.
I didn't want to interrupt her.

My cousin is gay; I always tell him that in our family tree, he's in the fruit section.

I came from a real tough neighborhood. I bought a waterbed and found a guy at the bottom of it.

My wife had her drivers test the other day. She got 8 out of 10. The other 2 guys jumped clear.

I found there was only one way to look thin, hang out with fat people.

I told my wife the truth. I told her I was seeing a psychiatrist. Then she told me the truth: that she was seeing a psychiatrist, two plumbers, and a bartender.

During sex, my girlfriend always wants to talk to me. Just the other night she called me from a hotel.

…went to a bar for a few drinks. The bartender asked what I wanted. 'Surprise me', I said. So he showed me a naked picture of my wife.

I was such an ugly kid… when I played in the sandbox, the cat kept covering me up.

Demetri Martin

Born:
May 25, 1973, in New York, New York, USA.

Career:
Demetri Martin began his career in comedy when he dropped out of law school. He has said in interviews that he found studies boring and that he wanted to pursue a comedy-career instead.

His career started with him performing in clubs and in 2001, Martin caught his first big break in stand-up comedy when he appeared on Comedy Central's stand-up showcase Premium Blend. In 2003, he became a writer on Late Night with Conan O'Brien. In 2004, Martin had his own Comedy Central Presents stand-up special.

Martin appeared at the 2005 Edinburgh Festival Fringe in a show called These Are Jokes. Since late 2005, he has been credited as a contributor on The Daily Show.

Employee of the month is a good example of how somebody can be both a winner and a loser at the same time.

I wrapped my Christmas presents early this year, but I used the wrong paper. See, the paper I used said 'Happy Birthday' on it. I didn't want to waste it so I just wrote 'Jesus' on it.

I got some new pajamas with pockets in 'em. Which is great, because before that, I used to have to hold stuff when I slept.

'Sort of' is such a harmless thing to say. Sort of. It's just a filler. Sort of - it doesn't really mean anything. But after certain things, sort of means everything. Like after 'I love you' or 'You're going to live' or 'It's a boy.'

I think vests are all about protection. You know what I mean? Like a lifevest protects you from from drowning and bullet-proof vests protect you from getting shot and the sweater-vest protects you from pretty girls.

I was making pancakes the other day and a fly flew into the kitchen. And that's when I realized that a spatula is a lot like a fly-swatter. And a crushed fly is a lot like a blueberry. And a roommate is a lot like a fly eater.

Swimming is a confusing sport, because sometimes you do it for fun, and other times you do it to not die.

The worst time to have a heart attack is during a game of charades.

I was at a party, and I saw a guy with a leather jacket, and I thought, 'That's cool'. Then I saw a guy with a leather vest and I thought, 'That's not cool'. It was then that I realized what coolness is all about... leather sleeves.

Dolphins are considered friendly animals, but I bet some of them are real jerks.

I bought a dictionary. First thing I did was, I looked up the word 'dictionary', and it said 'you're an asshole'.

David Letterman

Born:
April 12, 1947 in Indianapolis, Indiana.

Career:
Letterman started working in television on the 1970's, as a TV-announcer and weather man among other things. In the mid 1970's, he started writing material for sitcoms. He also began performing stand-up comedy at The Comedy Store. He was eventually discovered by talent scouts for The Tonight Show Starring Johnny Carson. In 1977, he started participating in the legendary show and he became a regular guest. The audience liked Letterman so much, that he got his own daytime talk show: The David Letterman Show. The show flopped and was cancelled after a few months. But in 1982, the show that made Letterman to one of our time's greatest talk show hosts started: Late Night with David Letterman. In 1992, Johnny Carson announced that he was retiring from hosting his show and many expected David Letterman to replace him. Contrary to everyone's beliefs, it was the competition; Jay Leno, who got the hosting job. The loss made Letterman leave NBC to start Late Show with David Letterman on CBS.

Letterman has been rewarded with numerous awards, such as American Comedy Award and Emmy Awards.

Congratulations are in order for Woody Allen - he and Soon Yi have a brand new baby daughter. It's all part of Woody's plan to grow his own wives.

Experts say that Iraq may have nuclear weapons. That's bad news - they may have a nuclear bomb. Now the good news is that they have to drop it with a camel.

President Bush says he needs a month off to unwind. Unwind? When the hell does this guy wind?

USA Today has come out with a new survey - apparently, three out of every four people make up 75% of the population.

George Carlin

Born:
May 12, 1937, in Bronx, New York, USA.

Career:
Carlin has worked with comedy for 40 years. He's often viewed as one of the most influential stand-up comedians of the late 20th century. Carlin dropped out of school when he was 17 years old and joined the Air Force as a radar mechanic. During his time at the Air Force, he started working as a DJ on the local radio station. That's where he met station's newsman Jack Burns. The two of them formed a comedian duo and moved to Hollywood to perform in local clubs. The duo launched his comedy-career and performed at Tonight Show Starring Johnny Carson, among others.

Today, Carlin is famous for his 'Seven Dirty Words You Can't Say on Radio or Television', which he was arrested for in 1972 for violating obscenity laws. In 1975, Carlin became the first host of NBC's Saturday Night Live.

Carlin has done a lot of HBO specials and also written best-seller books. In 1997, Carlin was honored at the Aspen Comedy Festival with a retrospective George Carlin: 40 Years of Comedy hosted by Jon Stewart.

When someone is impatient and says, 'I haven't got all day,' I always wonder, How can that be? How can you not have all day?

What if there were no hypothetical questions?

Death is caused by swallowing small amounts of saliva over a long period of time.

Fighting for peace is like screwing for virginity.

I would never want to be a member of a group whose symbol was a guy nailed to two pieces of wood.

The main reason Santa is so jolly is because he knows where all the bad girls live.

Honesty may be the best policy, but it's important to remember that apparently, by elimination, dishonesty is the second-best policy.

Rosanne Barr

Born:
November 3, 1952, in Salt Lake City, Utah, USA.

Career:
Barr dropped out of high school when she was 17 years old. During her teenage years, she worked as a dishwasher and waitress at a local restaurant. It is said that the guests at the restaurants enjoyed Barr's humor so much, that they encouraged her to become a comedian. I the early 1980's, she began performing at stand-up clubs. She quickly established herself as one of the most appreciated entertainers. In 1983, she left Denver to pursue happiness in Hollywood. She quickly landed a gig at the Comedy Store and during a rehearsal, she was spotted by a talent-scout, which lead to her first performance at The Tonight Show Starring Johnny Carson.

After participating in the legendary TV-show, Barr got her own stand-up comedy HBO show, On Location: The Roseanne Barr Show. Soon followed what she's most famous for, the sitcom Roseanne. This aired for nine seasons.

Roseanne has received numerous awards, including an Emmy, several People's Choice Awards, Golden Globes, and an American Comedy Award.

Women complain about premenstrual syndrome, but I think of it as the only time of the month that I can be myself.

Experts say you should never hit your children in anger. When is a good time? When you're feeling festive?

Men can read maps better than women. Cause only the male mind could conceive of one inch equalling a hundred miles.

When my husband comes home, if the kids are still alive, I figure I've done my job.

My hope is that gays will be running the world, because then there would be no war. Just a greater emphasis on military apparel.

The quickest way to a man's heart is through his chest.

I'm not going to vacuum 'til Sears makes one you can ride on.

I had left home (like all Jewish girls) in order to eat pork and take birth control pills. When I first shared an intimate evening with my husband I was swept away by the passion (so dormant inside myself) of a long and tortured existence. The physical cravings I had tried so hard to deny finally and ultimately sated... but enough about the pork.

My husband complained to me. He said 'I can't even remember when we last had sex', and I said, 'Well I can and that's why we ain't doin' it.'

Denis Leary

Born:
August 18, 1957, in Worcester, Massachusetts, USA.

Career:
Leary started his career as a stand-up comedian in Boston in the 1980's. He performed in several local clubs and he also wrote and appeared on a local comedy series. In 1990, he lived in the UK for a while and that's where he wrote the show No cure for cancer. The show became his big break. At this point, he was also doing promos for MTV, which made him popular with the larger audience.

During the 1990's, he also started working as an actor. In 1997, Leary taped his second stand-up show, Denis Leary: Lock 'n Load on HBO.

Leary was also nominated for an Outstanding Writing Emmy in 2005 and Outstanding Lead Actor Emmys in 2006 and 2007.

Most people think life sucks, and then you die. Not me. I beg to differ. I think life sucks, then you get cancer, then your dog dies, your wife leaves you, the cancer goes into remission, you get a new dog, you get remarried, you owe ten million dollars in medical bills but you work hard for thirty-five years and you pay it back and then -- one day -- you have a massive stroke, your whole right side is paralyzed, you have to limp along the streets and speak out of the left side of your mouth and drool but you go into rehabilitation and regain the power to walk and the power to talk and then -- one day -- you step off a curb at Sixty-seventh street, and BANG you get hit by a city bus and then you die. Maybe.

I would never do crack... I would never do a drug named after a part of my own ass, okay?

The best pitch I ever heard about cocaine was back in the early eighties when a street dealer followed me down the sidewalk going: I got some great blow man. I got the stuff that killed Belushi.

Jerry Lewis has been married twenty times. He gets married on a Tuesday, they find his wife dead in a swimming pool on Thursday. Maybe if you married someone who's old enough to swim next time, OK Jerry?

I recently read an interview in Rolling Stone, where he advocated that people should not do drugs, KEITH RICHARDS said that we should not do drugs. Keith, we can't do anymore drugs, BECAUSE YOU ALREADY FUCKIN' DID THEM ALL! There's none left, we have to wait until you die so we can smoke you're ashes, alright!

Mix of good quotes

Rosie o donnell

Stop at a drug store, buy a condom, and put it over your head. If you act like a dick, you might as well dress like one.

Sue Kolinsky

I would love to speak a foreign language but I can't.
So I grew hair under my arms instead.

Roger Simon

The reason most people play golf is to wear clothes they would not be caught dead in otherwise.

Peter cook

I became a coal minor. I managed to get through the mining exams. They're, eh, not very rigorous. They only ask you one question, 'Who are you?' and I got seventy-five percent on that.

Carol Leifer

I'm not into working out. My philosophy: No pain, no pain.

Ed Bluestone

I have a great diet. You're allowed to eat anything you want, but you must eat it with naked fat people.

Ray Romano

Men don't care what's on TV.
They only care what else is on TV.

Everyone should have kids. They are the greatest joy in the world. But they are also terrorists. You'll realize this as soon as they are born, and they start using sleep deprivation to break you.

Monica Piper

A man on a date wonders if he'll get lucky.
The woman knows.

Juries scare me. I don't want to put my faith in 12 people who weren't smart enough to get out of jury duty.

Dave Henry

Nothing can burst your fatherly bubble faster than hearing your daughter come home from a date and saying, 'Some nights I don't know why I even bother to wear panties.'

Daniel Lybra

Two guys walk into a bar. You'd think one of them would have seen it.

J.D. California

The worlds talles dwarf is named Marvin and he's from Michigan. He's six foot one inch tall.

Sex is the reason they invented babies.

Bruce Baum

I don't kill flies but I like to mess with their minds. I hold them above globes. They freak out and yell, 'Whoa, I'm way too high!'

Michael McShane

I'm a psychic amnesiac. I know in advance what I'll forget.

Jeff Stilson

I had a linguistics professor who said that it's man's ability to use language that makes him the dominant species on the planet. That may be. But I think there's one other thing that separates us from animals. We aren't afraid of vaccuum cleaners.

'Delivery' is the wrong word to describe the childbearing process. Delivery is: 'Here's your pizza. Takes 30 minutes or less.' 'Exorcism' I think, is more apt: 'Please! Get the hell out of my body!'

Adam Sandler

Chemistry can be a good and bad thing. Chemistry is good when you make love with it. Chemistry is bad when you make crack with it.

Dave Barry

Dogs feel very strongly that they should always go with you in the car, in case the need should arise for them to bark violently at nothing right in your ear.

Fishing is boring, unless you catch an actual fish, and then it is disgusting.

Camping is nature's way of promoting the motel business.

Life is anything that dies when you stomp on it.

The word 'user' is the word used by the computer professional when they mean idiot.

Dave Barry

Gravity is a contributing factor in nearly 73 percent of all accidents involving falling objects.

It always rains on tents. Rainstorms will travel thousands of miles, against prevailing winds for the opportunity to rain on a tent.

It is a scientific fact that your body will not absorb cholesterol if you take it from another person's plate.

It is a well-documented fact that guys will not ask for directions. This is a biological thing. This is why it takes several million sperm cells... to locate a female egg, despite the fact that the egg is, relative to them, the size of Wisconsin.

Scientists now believe that the primary biological function of breasts is to make males stupid.

Dave allen

I'm an atheist...thank God.

Robert Townsend

Consultants are people who borrow your watch and tell you what time it is, and then walk off with the watch.

Paul Rodriguez

Sometimes I think war is God's way of teaching us geography

What's wrong about eating cows? What do you think god made them for? Their big, their stupid, their delicious. You want more reasons? I never met an animal more prepared to die than a cow. Next time you go to the farm look at a cow in the eyes, it is begging you for a bullet.

Erma Bombeck

I come from a family where gravy is considered a beverage.

Lynda Montgomery

Why does Sea World have a seafood restaurant? I'm halfway through my fishburger and I realize, Oh my God, I could be eating a slow learner.

Mike Binder

I date this girl for two years and then the nagging starts:
I wanna know your name...

Billy crystal

Women need a reason to have sex. Men just need a place.

Larry David

When I was living in New York and didn't have a penny to my name, I would walk around the streets and occasionally I would see an alcove or something. And I'd think, that'll be good, that'll be a good spot for me when I'm homeless.

I'll have a vanilla... one of those vanilla bullshit things. You know, whatever you want, some vanilla bullshit latte cappa thing. Whatever you got.

Stephen fry

I think animal testing is a terrible idea; they get all nervous and give the wrong answers.

A cousin of mine who was a casualty surgeon in Manhattan tells me that he and his colleagues had a one-word nick-name for bikers: Donors. Rather chilling.

Whoppi goldberg

Whenever women are together for more than two days they talk about their periods.

Kelsey grammer

Joy, christmas Eve. By this time tomorrow, millions of Americans, knee deep in tinsel and wrapping paper, will utter those heartfelt words: 'Is this all I got?'

Will ferrell

98 percent of us will die at some point in our lives.

I have only been funny about seventy four per cent of the time. Yes I think that is right. Seventy-four per cent of the time.

Spike Milligan

I have the body of an eighteen year old.
I keep it in the fridge.

A sure cure for seasickness is to sit under a tree.

All I ask is the chance to prove that money
can't make me happy.

Whitney Brown

I'm not a vegetarian because I love animals. I am a vegetarian because I hate plants.

I'm not an athiest. How can you not believe in something that doesn't exist? That's way too convoluted for me.

Carrie Snow

Having a male gynecologist is like going to an auto mechanic who doesn't own a car.

James Knowles

It appears that President Bush's concept of attacking a country 'before' it becomes a threat has been adopted by society in general. Yesterday I got an e-mail message from the entire female population of Ohio, requesting that I not ask them for a date.

Chester Ingraham

My wife always thinks it's cute when the baby throws up on me. But when it's the other way around, she gets all huffy and accuses me of being drunk.

Larry Hollister

I'm feeling a little guilty. Today was the first day of the rest of my life, and all I did was drink Old Milwaukee and watch the Cartoon Network.

Corrina Bunch

Relationships should come with those little black boxes that airplanes have. That way, when they crash and burn, we'd actually get some answers.

Scott Leiter

I know the difference between sadist and masochist... but you're going to have to beat it out of me.

Jimmy Shubert

Women might be able to fake orgasms. But men can fake whole relationships.

Francois Morency

What are the three words guaranteed to humiliate men everywhere? 'Hold my purse.'

Linda Ellerbee

If men can run the world, why can't they stop wearing neck-ties? How intelligent is it to start the day by tying a little noose around your neck?

Jake Johansen

A lady came up to me on the street and pointed at my suede jacket. 'You know a cow was murdered for that jacket?' she sneered. I replied in a psychotic tone, 'I didn't know there were any witnesses. Now I'll have to kill you too.'

Warren Hutcherson

I was court-ordered to Alcoholics Anonymous on television. Pretty much blows the hell out of the second A, wouldn't you say?

In elementary school, in case of fire you have to line up quietly in a single file line from smallest to tallest. What is the logic? Do tall people burn slower?

Sue Murphy

Did you ever walk in a room and forget why you walked in?
I think that's how dogs spend their lives.

Joel Lindley

I was a bank teller. That was a great job. I was bringing home
$450,000 a week.

Janeane Garofalo

I guess I just prefer to see the dark side of things. The glass is always half empty. And cracked. And I just cut my lip on it. And chipped a tooth.

Bob Ettinger

Relationships are hard. It's like a full-time job, and we should treat it like one. If your boyfriend or girlfriend wants to leave you, they should give you two weeks' notice. There should be severance pay, and before they leave you, they should have to find you a temp.

Kevin Meaney

I've been doing the Fonda workout: the Peter Fonda workout. That's where I wake up, take a hit of acid, smoke a joint, and go to my sister's house and ask her for money.

Rich Jeni

There are only two reasons to sit in the back row of an airplane: Either you have diarrhea, or you're anxious to meet people who do.

Wendy Liebman

I went to the 30th reunion of my preschool. I didn't want to go, because I've put on like a hundred pounds.

I've learned that you cannot make someone love you. All you can do is stalk them and hope they panic and give in.

I've been on so many blind dates, I should get a free dog.

Rich Jeni

Honesty is the key to a relationship. If you can fake that, you're in.

Tracy Smith

I wanted to make it really special on Valentine's day, so I tied my boyfriend up. And for three solid hours I watched whatever I wanted on TV.

Brad Wilkerson

I've made provisions in my will to be buried with a roll of breath mints. I figure if I should somehow become part of a zombie army roaming the earth, I may want something minty fresh to take the taste of brains out of my mouth.

Sure, companies say they're sensitive to their employees' cultural heritages, but show up on casual Friday wearing a necklace made from the ears of your vanquished enemies and all hell breaks loose.

Curtis Stoddard

If those Davy Crockett coonskin caps ever come back in style I'm a genius. If they don't, I'm just another guy with a garage full of carcasses.

Margaret Smith

I took my parents back to the airport today.
They leave tomorrow.

I don't visit my parents often because Delta Airlines won't wait in the yard while I run in.

Fran Lebowitz

My favorite animal is steak.

I figure you have the same chance of winning the lottery whether you play or not.

In real life, I assure you, there is no such thing as algebra.

Remember that as a teenager you are at the last stage of your life when you will be happy to hear that the phone is for you.

Food is an important part of a balanced diet.